"Like someone who has uncovered a forgotten treasure, Bill Huebsch returns again and again to the documents and spirit of Vatican II and brings forth the great work of that momentous event in history for all to see and remember. The prayer services in this collection capture the major themes and developments of the Council. They, like the documents invite a lectio divina.

"The services are just right for use by parish pastoral councils, committees, and by any group who gathers to become church."

Edmund F. Gordon
Director of Religious Education
Diocese of Wilmington, DE

"Since the close of Vatican Council II in 1965, its documents have been endlessly quoted and paraphrased in articles, homilies, books, and kitchen table discussions; earnest people have appealed to them to support their theological or pastoral positions. But over the years the spirit of these official papers, which recapture the freshness of the gospels and are profound in their pastoral implications, has been increasingly ignored and even contested. But have the words and the spirit of these inspired writings really seeped into our souls?

"Bill Huebsch, who has already given us a most readable and inspiring paraphrase of these documents, now gives us 18 prayer services based on the major themes of the council, such as the eucharist, the church in the world today, the role of the laity, religious liberty, the call to justice and peace, the role of conscience, baptism, and the universal call to holiness. The prayers and reflections of these services rightly center around gospel readings and readings from Vatican II documents. Communal prayer using *People of God at Prayer* is a step toward rekindling the spirit of Vatican II and reestablishing its rightful place in daily life."

John van Bemmel
Author, *Prayers About Everyday Stuff:
Off the Cuff and From the Heart*
Co-Author, *100 Prayers for Making Faith Connections*

"Bill Huebsch's writing is like a breath of fresh air. He knows how to present complicated theological insights in simple and understandable terms. That's what he does in *People of God at Prayer.* So those who use this book have a double advantage: they will pray meaningfully and they will learn or re-learn the teachings of Vatican II."

Gwen Costello
Editor, *Religion Teacher's Journal*
Author, *Praying with the Saints*

Bill Huebsch

People
of God at
Prayer

18 SERVICES
in the Spirit of Vatican II

TWENTY-THIRD PUBLICATIONS
BAYARD 🙂 Mystic, CT 06355

Second Printing 2003

The Scripture passages contained herein are from the New Revised Standard Version of the Bible, copyright © 1989, by the Division of Christian Education of the National Council of Churches of Christ in the U.S.A. All rights reserved.

Twenty-Third Publications/Bayard
185 Willow Street
P.O. Box 180
Mystic, CT 06355
(860) 536-2611
(800) 321-0411

ISBN:1-58595-012-0
Library of Congress Catalog Card Number: 99-75804
Printed in the U.S.A.

Contents

People of God at Prayer

Introduction
to the Prayers

Ever since I first encountered
    the powerful and spirit-filled documents of Vatican II,
    I have hoped to see a day
        when they would be celebrated
    in our parishes and homes
        through prayer.
Reading these documents in their original translations
    is itself a great inspiration.
Knowing the story of their provenance
    is also tremendously helpful.
And understanding the hundreds of postconciliar developments
    relating to each document
    is certainly essential to us.

But there is also a time to pause
    and allow our prayer to be filled
    with the power of what happened at Vatican II.

There the Holy Spirit became present
    through a miraculous gathering
    of the body of the world's bishops
    in union with the bishop of Rome,
        together with representatives
            from Protestant,
            Orthodox,
            and Anglican churches,
        in the presence of our Jewish brothers and sisters,
        with regard for people of all the world's many Faiths,
        and even with a nod to those people
            who have no faith at all
            but are, nonetheless, of good will.

Here we saw, gathered in one place,
    the many expressions of the people of God.
Here we heard expressed the desire for peace,
    for justice,
    for unity,
    and for holiness,
        which are so basic to all humans.
Here the pope and bishops raised up the hopes of the world

for a new day and a fresh spirit in the Church.
Indeed, this council has been called
        "the Advent liturgy of the new millennium."

These prayers draw, as all prayer does,
        from our Sacred Scriptures.
But they also draw from the council documents,
        not by quoting them directly,
        but through psalm-like reflections
        inspired by the documents themselves.
These prayers are meant to bring us closer
        to the work of God
                in our lives and in our Church.
They are meant to highlight
        our experience of God's work in our day,
        especially as we encounter it
        through the inspired outcomes
                of the Second Vatican Council.

Indeed, there is precedence in the Church
        for the use of non-biblical readings
        in our prayer.
The "General Instruction of the Liturgy of the Hours,"
        paragraph 159 and following,
        provides some insight to this.
"In accordance with the tradition of the Roman Church,"
        it says,
        "the Office of Readings provides,
                after the biblical reading,
                a reading from the Fathers
                        or Church writers…."

"Besides the readings assigned to each day
        in the Liturgy of the Hours,"
        it goes on to say in paragraph 161,
                "there is an optional lectionary
                with a larger selection of readings,
                in order that the treasures of the Church's tradition
                        may be more widely available
                        to those who pray…."

With this very purpose in mind, then,
        I have prepared this book of prayers
        to help us celebrate Vatican II
                and to help us proclaim its spirit
                to one another.

For the Church, the Body of Christ

Leader   (using these or similar words)
Let's all take a moment of silence
here in the midst of our busy lives
     in order to collect the events of today
     and bring ourselves, body and soul,
          into this gathering.

Pause for a moment of sacred silence.

Leader   (using these or similar words)
Friends, we now gather here as God's family,
and we know that we are, indeed, the Body of Christ
     whenever we gather like this in his name.
May we enter into this time now
     conscious of this high calling
     and open to God's voice within and among us.

All   **In the name of God, Amen.**

Leader   (Invite all to listen to, sing, or recite an opening song-prayer.)

First Reading

Reader   A reading from the Gospel of Mark (Mk 4:30–32):
He also said, "With what can we compare the kingdom of God, or what parable
will we use for it? It is like a mustard seed, which, when sown upon the ground, is
the smallest of all the seeds on earth; yet when it is sown it grows up and becomes
the greatest of all shrubs, and puts forth large branches, so that the birds of the air
can make nests in its shade."

The word of the Lord.

All   **Thanks be to God for these words of Scripture!**

Second Reading

Reader   A reflection based on the Constitution on the Sacred Liturgy
from the Second Vatican Council:

We now proclaim that Jesus Christ
      has freed us from our sins
      has saved us from death,
      and has brought us into the reign of God.
The ongoing work of Christ's saving power
      takes place through the sacraments,
      especially the Mass.

By baptism we are implanted in the very soul of Christ,
      in the paschal mystery.
We are made daughters and sons
      through adoption
      and as often as we eat the Lord's supper,
      we proclaim this mystery
      and live in the power of the Spirit.
From the earliest days onward, then,
      the church has never stopped celebrating the Eucharist
      and proclaiming the Scriptures.
In Christ, we live in the power of God.
(Article 6)

From the word of the Church.

All   **Thanks be to God for this teaching.**

Prayer of the Church

Leader   Jesus, Lord and source of our lives,
                we now come to you in prayer.

All   **With our whole heart we pray to you.**

Leader   Form within us the desire to be your Body.

All   **Lead us to see the world with eyes of faith.**

Leader   May we in the Church be a sign to the world of your love.

All   **May the church we love be holy.**

Leader   And may the people of the world see in us
                the holiness promised by you.

All   **May all live in peace.**

Leader	And for each other here we pray that we might be earnest in our search for truth and fair in our judgments of others.
All	**May we seek the truth and be fair in all we do and say.** **Amen. Amen. Amen.**

Blessing

Leader	May God who loves us deeply…
All	**O God, we love you without end.**
Leader	May the Spirit who is our guide…
All	**O Spirit, we listen to your voice.**
Leader	And may Jesus Christ in whose name we gather…
All	**O Jesus, we adore you.**
Leader	now bless us, direct us, and be with us in love, now and forever.
All	**We receive your blessing with full hearts.** **Amen. Amen. Amen.**

Closing Prayer

Leader	(using these or similar words) O God, we know that you are with us and you guide us in all we do. We are ready now to be your Body and to allow your Spirit to lead us in your ways.
All	**In the name of God, Amen.**
Leader	(Invite all to listen to, sing, or recite a closing song-prayer.)

In Thanksgiving for Our Call to Baptism

Leader   (using these or similar words)
            Let's all take a moment of silence
            here in the midst of our busy lives
                    to collect the events of today
                    and bring ourselves, body and soul,
                            into this gathering.

Pause for a moment of sacred silence.

Leader   (using these or similar words)
            Friends, we now gather here as God's family,
            baptized as we are into Christ
                    and made ready for ministry
                    in the church and in the world.
            May we enter into this time now
                    conscious of our high calling
                    and open to God's voice within and among us.

All   **In the name of God, Amen.**

Leader   (Invite all to listen to, sing, or recite an opening song-prayer.)

First Reading

Reader   A reading from the Gospel of Matthew (Mt 28:17–20):
            When they saw him, they worshiped him; but some doubted. And Jesus came and
            said to them, "All authority in heaven and on earth has been given to me. Go
            therefore and make disciples of all nations, baptizing them in the name of the
            Father and of the Son and of the Holy Spirit, and teaching them to obey every-
            thing that I have commanded you. And remember, I am with you always, to the
            end of the age."

            The word of the Lord.

All   **Thanks be to God for these words of Scripture!**

Second Reading

Reader   A reflection based on the Decree on the Laity
from the Second Vatican Council:

The right and duty of laypeople
to work in the mission of the Church
comes directly from Christ himself.
Through baptism
all are brought into the family of Christ,
and with the power of the Spirit at confirmation,
all are assigned to work
all are called to animate the world
with the Spirit of Christ.
Throughout our lives, then,
baptism forms the foundation
of our apostolate.
(Article 3)

From the word of the Church.

All   **Thanks be to God for this teaching.**

Prayer of the Church

Leader   O God, you have called us to baptism in Christ…

All   **We embrace our baptisms with faith.**

Leader   In that calling you give us the grace to minister to others…

All   **And in our ministry to announce the Good News.**

Leader   We now stand before you ready for this work
and in need of your wisdom, strength, courage, and love.

All   **O God, give us your love.**

Leader   May the Church prepare the world to see you,

All   **And may the world respond in faith.**

Leader   And for each other here
we pray that we might be earnest in our search for truth
and fair in our judgments of others.

All	May we seek the truth and be fair in all we do and say. **Amen. Amen. Amen.**

Blessing

Leader	May God who loves us deeply…
All	**O God, we love you without end.**
Leader	May the Spirit who is our guide…
All	**O Spirit, we listen to your voice.**
Leader	And may Jesus Christ in whose name we gather…
All	**O Jesus, we adore you.**
Leader	now bless us, direct us, and be with us in love, now and forever.
All	**We receive your blessing with full hearts.** **Amen. Amen. Amen.**

Closing Prayer

Leader	(using these or similar words)
	O God, we know that you are with us
	     and that you guide us in all we do.
	We are ready now to be your baptized people,
	     touching the world with love.

All	**In the name of God, Amen.**
Leader	(Invite all to listen to, sing, or recite a closing song-prayer.)

In Celebration of Our Universal Call to Holiness

Leader   (using these or similar words)
              Let's all take a moment of silence
              here in the midst of our busy lives
                    in order to collect the events of today
                    and bring ourselves, body and soul,
                          into this gathering.

Pause for a moment of sacred silence.

Leader   (using these or similar words)
              Friends, we now gather here as God's family,
              the people chosen to live in holiness.
              May we enter into this time now
                    conscious of our high calling
                    and open to God's voice within and among us.

All   **In the name of God, Amen.**

Leader   (Invite all to listen to, sing, or recite an opening song-prayer.)

First Reading

Reader   A reading from the first letter of Peter (1 Pt 1:13–16):
              Therefore prepare your minds for action; discipline yourselves; set all your hope on
              the grace that Jésus Christ will bring you when he is revealed. Like obedient children,
              do not be conformed to the desires that you formerly had in ignorance.
              Instead, as he who called you is holy, be holy yourselves in all your conduct; for it
              is written, "You shall be holy, for I am holy."

              The word of the Lord.

All   **Thanks be to God for these words of Scripture!**

Second Reading

Reader   A reflection based on the Dogmatic Constitution on the Church

9

from the Second Vatican Council:

No matter what your condition of life,
    no matter who you are
    or what you do,
        Christ is calling you to be holy.
    In fact, the Spirit is even now
    moving you interiorly
        to love God more deeply
        and serve God more fully.
    We have been made sons and daughters of God
    through baptism
    and now we share in the divine life.
This means that we are truly made holy,
    we are truly called to live accordingly.
We are among the saints,
    God's chosen ones,
        beloved of God,
        called to be meek,
           to be kind,
           and to be loving.
God's mercy is upon us. Amen.
(Article 40)

From the word of the Church.

All   **Thanks be to God for this teaching.**

Prayer of the Church

Leader   We thank you, O God, for calling each of us
to live in holiness and love.
May we now embrace this calling with faith.

All   **And may we live in love.**

Leader   We believe your Spirit fills us
and empowers us to respond to your presence.

All   **May your spirit kindle in us the fire of your love.**

Leader   We have been touched and healed by Christ
who lives with us now and forever.

All   **Lord Jesus, fill us with grace
and lead each of us to a holy life. Amen.**

Blessing

Leader	May God who loves us deeply…
All	**O God, we love you without end.**
Leader	May the Spirit who is our guide…
All	**O Spirit, we listen to your voice.**
Leader	And may Jesus Christ in whose name we gather…
All	**O Jesus, we adore you.**
Leader	now bless us, direct us, and be with us in love, now and forever.
All	**We receive your blessing with full hearts. Amen. Amen. Amen.**

Closing Prayer

Leader	(using these or similar words) O God, we know that you are with us and you guide all we are about to do. We are ready now to live as your holy people touched by the Spirit and filled with love in Christ.
All	**In the name of God, Amen.**
Leader	(Invite all to listen to, sing, or recite a closing song-prayer.)

In Thanksgiving for the Eucharist

Leader (using these or similar words)
Let's all take a moment of silence
here in the midst of our busy lives
in order to collect the events of today
and bring ourselves, body and soul,
into this gathering.

Pause for a moment of sacred silence.

Leader (using these or similar words)
Friends, we now gather here as God's family,
the people chosen to be part of the Body of Christ
and at the same time to receive
the Body of Christ.
May we enter into this time now
conscious of our high calling
and open to God's voice within and among us.

All **In the name of God, Amen.**

Leader (Invite all to listen to, sing, or recite an opening song-prayer.)

First Reading

Reader A reading from the Gospel of John (Jn 13:3–9)
Jesus, knowing that the Father had given all things into his hands, and that he had come from God and was going to God, got up from the table, took off his outer robe, and tied a towel around himself. Then he poured water into a basin and began to wash the disciples' feet and to wipe them with the towel that was tied around him. He came to Simon Peter, who said to him, "Lord, are you going to wash my feet?" Jesus answered, "You do not know now what I am doing, but later you will understand." Peter said to him, "You will never wash my feet." Jesus answered, "Unless I wash you, you have no share with me." Simon Peter said to him, "Lord, not my feet only but also my hands and my head!"

The word of the Lord.

All **Thanks be to God for these words of Scripture!**

Second Reading

Reader   A reflection based on the Constitution on the Sacred Liturgy
from the Second Vatican Council:

The Christian life which we all strive to live
    finds it apex and goal
    in the Liturgy of the Church.
And likewise, the Liturgy is also
    the very source of our life to begin with.
Celebrating the liturgy sets us on fire
    with God's love
    and charges us up for our daily lives.
And among all the liturgical celebrations
    in which we take part
    over the course of our lives,
        clearly the most central
        is the Eucharist!
Here God's promise to be with us forever
    is made plain and renewed.
Here Christ's love for us
    is expressed and experienced.
And here the Spirit touches us
    and makes us God's priestly people.

Indeed, then,
    because this is so important to us
    everyone should make him or herself ready
        when they come to celebrate.
We should not take it lightly
    or allow it to become routine.
And we should not think that merely following the rubrics
    is enough either.
Rather, we should enter the Eucharistic liturgy
    with full hearts
    and ample preparation
        so that its power is released
        and the world is renewed in love.
(Articles 10 & 11)

From the word of the Church.

All   **Thanks be to God for this teaching.**

Prayer of the Church

Leader   Jesus, Lord and Giver of Life,
we join our hearts in gratitude now.

All   **Thank you for giving us your body.**

Leader   Nothing we do or say together is more powerful
than when we stand at your table in Faith.

All   **Thank you for giving us the Eucharist.**

Leader   Help us, we pray, to open our hearts and our doors
to allow in those whom you call to yourself.

All   **May we become your body for them.**

Leader   And may all who gather in your name,
may all people who believe in you,

All   **Gather in unity and put division aside.
Amen. Again we say, Amen!**

Blessing

Leader   May God who loves us deeply…

All   **O God, we love you without end.**

Leader   May the Spirit who is our guide…

All   **O Spirit, we listen to your voice.**

Leader   And may Jesus Christ in whose name we gather…

All   **O Jesus, we adore you.**

Leader   now bless us,
direct us,
and be with us in love, now and forever.

All   **We receive your blessing with full hearts.
Amen. Amen. Amen.**

Closing Prayer

Leader   (using these or similar words)
O God, we know that you are with us
and you guide all we are about to do.
We are ready now to allow you to mold our hearts
     and shape us into the community
     which truly reflects your desire for the world.

All   **In the name of God, Amen.**

Leader   (Invite all to listen to, sing, or recite a closing song-prayer.)

In Thanksgiving for Divine Revelation

Leader (using these or similar words)
Let's all take a moment of silence
here in the midst of our busy lives
 in order to collect the events of today
 and bring ourselves, body and soul,
  into this gathering.

Pause for a moment of sacred silence.

Leader (using these or similar words)
Friends, we now gather here as God's family,
the people chosen to receive your revelation
 and witness that to the ends of the Earth.
May we enter into this time now
 conscious of our high calling
 and open to God's voice within and among us.

All **In the name of God, Amen.**

Leader (Invite all to listen to, sing, or recite an opening song-prayer.)

First Reading

Reader A reading from the second letter of Paul to Timothy (2 Tim 1:8–10)
Do not be ashamed, then, of the testimony about our Lord or of me his prisoner, but join with me in suffering for the gospel, relying on the power of God, who saved us and called us with a holy calling, not according to our works but according to his own purpose and grace. This grace was given to us in Christ Jesus before the ages began, but it has now been revealed through the appearing of our Savior Christ Jesus, who abolished death and brought life and immortality to light through the gospel.

The word of the Lord.

All **Thanks be to God for these words of Scripture!**

Second Reading

Reader   A reflection based on the Constitution on Divine Revelation
from the Second Vatican Council:

God desires that we humans
        come to know fully and completely
        what it means to live in divine love.
    This love in God
    is expressed in the Trinity's own love
    and to us it is unfathomable.
God calls us friends!
    How wonderful!
    How delightful for us!
By doing this, God helps us come closer
    even though God remains the infinitely Holy.

Thus God reveals God's own very Self to us
    not merely with words
    but also with great deeds.
Indeed, God's deeds throughout history
    make the doctrine plain to us
    while at the same time,
        the doctrine helps elaborate for us
        what we see in God's action among us.
And the most intimate and loving truth about God
    shines forth for us in Christ
    who sums up all God wishes to say to us.
(Article 2)

From the word of the Church.

All   **Thanks be to God for this teaching.**

Prayers for the Church   (choose one or compose one)

Leader   O God, you have revealed yourself to us
in the innermost recesses of our souls
and in the public forum of the Church.

All   **Lead us to recognize your word revealed in our time and place.**

Leader   You invite us to intimate companionship with you.

All   **You make us your friends and lovers.**

Leader	What we have seen and heard from you we now wish to share with others.
All	**We are your people.** **We go forth to tell everyone what we have seen.**
Leader	And in Christ you have made known to us all there is for us to know.
All	**Thank you for giving us Christ.** **Amen.**

Blessing

Leader	May God who loves us deeply…
All	**O God, we love you without end.**
Leader	May the Spirit who is our guide…
All	**O Spirit, we listen to your voice.**
Leader	And may Jesus Christ in whose name we gather…
All	**O Jesus, we adore you.**
Leader	now bless us, direct us, and be with us in love, now and forever.
All	**We receive your blessing with full hearts.** **Amen. Amen. Amen.**

Closing Prayer

Leader	(using these or similar words) O God, we know that you are with us and you guide all we are about to do. We are ready now to witness to your Word to the ends of the Earth.
All	**In the name of God, Amen.**
Leader	(Invite all to listen to, sing, or recite a closing song-prayer.)

For Religious Liberty
Around the World

Leader   (using these or similar words)
Let's all take a moment of silence
here in the midst of our busy lives
 in order to collect the events of today
 and bring ourselves, body and soul,
  into this gathering.

Pause for a moment of sacred silence.

Leader   (using these or similar words)
Friends, we now gather here as God's family,
the people given the freedom of the Children of God.
May we enter into this time now
 conscious of our high calling
 and open to God's voice within and among us.

All   **In the name of God, Amen.**

Leader   (Invite all to listen to, sing, or recite an opening song-prayer.)

First Reading

Reader   A reading from the Gospel of Mark (Mk 10:47–52)
When he heard that it was Jesus of Nazareth, he began to shout out and say,
"Jesus, Son of David, have mercy on me!" Many sternly ordered him to be quiet,
but he cried out even more loudly, "Son of David, have mercy on me!" Jesus stood
still and said, "Call him here." And they called the blind man, saying to him,
"Take heart; get up, he is calling you." So throwing off his cloak, he sprang up
and came to Jesus. Then Jesus said to him, "What do you want me to do for you?"
The blind man said to him, "My teacher, let me see again." Jesus said to him,
"Go; your faith has made you well." Immediately he regained his sight and followed
him on the way.

The word of the Lord.

All   **Thanks be to God for these words of Scripture!**

Second Reading

Reader   A reflection based on the Declaration on Religious Liberty
from the Second Vatican Council:

We hereby declare
    that each of us has a right
    to religious freedom.
We should all be immune from force
    by individuals,
    groups,
    or any other human power.
We should never be forced to act
    against our own convictions
    nor restrained from following
      our own consciences.
We have the right to a private life
    but also to associate with others
    who share our beliefs.
And this freedom of which we speak
    is based on the dignity of being human
    as we know it through God's own revelation.
Governments should provide societies
    which respect this
    everywhere in the world.
(Article 2)

From the word of the Church.

All   **Thanks be to God for this teaching.**

Prayer of the Church

Leader   O God, you have made us humans in your image
and given us freedom and responsibility.

All   **Freedom to love and responsibility to serve.**

Leader   Grant us now a new sense of dignity for all humanity
and the courage to speak on behalf of the unfree.

All   **Let us set all men and women free!**

Leader   We pray, too, for all those who suffer persecution
around the world.

All	May they hope in us.
	Amen. Again we say,
	may they hope in us. Amen!

Blessing

Leader	May God who loves us deeply…

All	O God, we love you without end.

Leader	May the Spirit who is our guide…

All	O Spirit, we listen to your voice.

Leader	And may Jesus Christ in whose name we gather…

All	O Jesus, we adore you.

Leader	now bless us,
	direct us,
	and be with us in love, now and forever.

All	We receive your blessing with full hearts.
	Amen. Amen. Amen.

Closing Prayer

Leader	(using these or similar words)
	O God, we know that you are with us
	and you guide all we are about to do.
	We are ready now to work for the freedom of all people
	all over the world
	with the courage our Faith provides.

All	In the name of God, Amen.

Leader	(Invite all to listen to, sing, or recite a closing song-prayer.)

For the Church in the Modern World

Leader   (using these or similar words)
Let's all take a moment of silence
here in the midst of our busy lives
    in order to collect the events of today
    and bring ourselves, body and soul,
        into this gathering.

Pause for a moment of sacred silence.

Leader   (using these or similar words)
Friends, we now gather here as God's family,
the people chosen to live in this world,
    in this day and age,
    with all our current situations
        of politics, economics, and life.
May we enter into this time now
    conscious of our high calling
    and open to God's voice within and among us.

All   **In the name of God, Amen.**

Leader   (Invite all to listen to, sing, or recite an opening song-prayer.)

First Reading

Reader   A reading from the Gospel of Matthew (Mt 25:37–40)
Then the righteous will answer him, "Lord, when was it that we saw you hungry and gave you food, or thirsty and gave you something to drink? And when was it that we saw you a stranger and welcomed you, or naked and gave you clothing? And when was it that we saw you sick or in prison and visited you?"

And the king will answer them, "Truly I tell you, just as you did it to one of the least of these who are members of my family, you did it to me."

The word of the Lord.

All   **Thanks be to God for these words of Scripture!**

Second Reading

Reader   A reflection based on the Pastoral Constitution on the Church
in the Modern World from the Second Vatican Council:

The joy and hope, the grief and anguish
     of the people of our time,
     especially the poor and afflicted
     this is the joy and hope,
         the grief and anguish,
         of the followers of Christ.
All the feelings of the human person,
     find expression in the hearts of Christians.
For we are united in Christ, after all,
     and we are bound together with each other,
         carrying an essential word
         to all of humankind for its salvation.
We in the Church are about the human situation
     for we are not without bodies
     and our bodies are created by God.
Human history unfolds before us
     complete with triumph and tragedy.
Only with God
     can it come to its intended goal:
         unity and love in Christ
         by the power of the Holy Spirit.
(Articles 1 & 2)

From the word of the Church.

All   **Thanks be to God for this teaching.**

Prayer of the Church

Leader   Jesus, Lord and Giver of Life
we come to you in faith seeking your grace.

All   **We come in faith.**

Leader   Empower us to know your will and serve you faithfully.

All   **Let your holy spirit abide with us now.**
Let your power fill us.

Leader   You call us with your voice to make our world

a garden of peace, love, and joy.

| All | **Give us the insight and courage to establish your reign on earth.** |

| Leader | You bring us together here with our weakness and frailty |

| All | **But you strengthen us for your work.**
May we sing your praises forever.
Amen. |

Blessing

| Leader | May God who loves us deeply… |

| All | **O God, we love you without end.** |

| Leader | May the Spirit who is our guide… |

| All | **O Spirit, we listen to your voice.** |

| Leader | And may Jesus Christ in whose name we gather… |

| All | **O Jesus, we adore you.** |

| Leader | now bless us,
direct us,
and be with us in love, now and forever. |

| All | **We receive your blessing with full hearts.**
Amen. Amen. Amen. |

Closing Prayer

| Leader | (using these or similar words)
O God, we know that you are with us
and you guide all we are about to do.
We are ready now to take up the work
    of being the Church
    in today's Modern World. |

| All | **In the name of God, Amen.** |

| Leader | (Invite all to listen to, sing, or recite a closing song-prayer.) |

For the Domestic Church

Leader (using these or similar words)
Let's all take a moment of silence
here in the midst of our busy lives
   in order to collect the events of today
   and bring ourselves, body and soul,
     into this gathering.

Pause for a moment of sacred silence.

Leader (using these or similar words)
Friends, we now gather here as God's family.
Each of us comes from our own household
   called to live our faith in our everyday lives.
May we enter into this time now
   conscious of this high calling
   and open to God's voice within and among us.

All **In the name of God, Amen.**

Leader (Invite all to listen to, sing, or recite an opening song-prayer.)

First Reading

Reader A reading from the first letter of John (1 Jn 2:9–14)
Whoever says, "I am in the light," while hating a brother or sister, is still in the darkness. Whoever loves a brother or sister lives in the light, and in such a person there is no cause for stumbling. But whoever hates another believer is in the darkness, walks in the darkness, and does not know the way to go, because the darkness has brought on blindness. I am writing to you, little children, because your sins are forgiven on account of his name. I am writing to you, fathers, because you know him who is from the beginning. I am writing to you, young people, because you have conquered the evil one. I write to you, children, because you know the Father. I write to you, fathers, because you know him who is from the beginning. I write to you, young people, because you are strong and the word of God abides in you, and you have overcome the evil one.

The word of the Lord.

All **Thanks be to God for these words of Scripture!**

Second Reading

Reader   A reflection based on the Pastoral Constitution on the Church
in the Modern World from the Second Vatican Council:

In a real sense
    the family is the school of life.
But in order for the household
    to provide this training ground,
    and to flower fully,
        it must be filled with affection.
It must be a place of love.

The role of the parents is essential in this.
Without underrating women's social advancement,
    time must be provided
    to allow mothers to care for their children
    and fathers to take their part as well.
Children should be raised with freedom,
    but also with discipline and faith.
Various generations come together
    in the Christian household
    in order to make this happen best.
(Article 52)

From the word of the Church.

All   **Thanks be to God for this teaching.**

Prayer of the Church

Leader   Jesus, Lord and Giver of Life,
we come to you in faith seeking your grace.

All   **We come in faith.**

Leader   Empower us to live our everyday lives at home
with the same faith we express in our parish celebrations.

All   **May your spirit guide us
to fill our lives with faith.**

Leader   And for this daily living we need your grace.

All   **Let your power fill us.**

Leader	You bring us together here with our weakness and frailty.
All	**But you strengthen us for our work.** **May we sing your praises forever.** **Amen.**

Blessing

Leader	May God who loves us deeply…
All	**O God, we love you without end.**
Leader	May the Spirit who is our guide…
All	**O Spirit, we listen to your voice.**
Leader	And may Jesus Christ in whose name we gather…
All	**O Jesus, we adore you.**
Leader	now bless us, direct us, and be with us in love, now and forever.
All	**We receive your blessing with full hearts.** **Amen. Amen. Amen.**

Closing Prayer

Leader	(using these or similar words) O God, we know that you are with us and you guide all we are about to do. We are ready now to be your domestic church living every day in your name and filling our homes with your love.
All	**In the name of God, Amen.**
Leader	(Invite all to listen to, sing, or recite a closing song-prayer.)

For Clarity
of Conscience

Leader   (using these or similar words)
Let's all take a moment of silence
here in the midst of our busy lives
    in order to collect the events of today
    and bring ourselves, body and soul,
       into this gathering.

Pause for a moment of sacred silence.

Leader   (using these or similar words)
Friends, we now gather here as God's family,
a people given the inner light of our consciences
    as our personal sanctuary with you.
May we enter into this time now
    conscious of our high calling
    and open to God's voice within and among us.

All   **In the name of God, Amen.**

Leader   (Invite all to listen to, sing, or recite an opening song-prayer.)

First Reading

Reader   A reading from the letter of Paul to the Romans (Rm 2:14–16)
When people who do not have the law naturally do what the law requires, then,
even though they don't "possess" the law strictly speaking, they may be said to
"be" the law. They show that what the law requires is written on their hearts.
Their own conscience bears witness to the law in the dialogue of their hearts and
they will be excused on the day when, according to my gospel, God, through Jesus
Christ, will judge the secret thoughts of all. (Note: this is not NRSV; it's my own
translation. BH)

The word of the Lord.

All   **Thanks be to God for these words of Scripture!**

Second Reading

Reader   A reflection based on The Pastoral Constitution on the Church
in the Modern World from the Second Vatican Council:

Deep within each of us
     there is a voice which calls us
         to do what is loving
         and to avoid what is evil.
This voice directs us according to a law
     which we have not made up ourselves,
     a law which seems to come
         from somewhere beyond us all.
Nevertheless, this eternal, divine law
     is one which we must obey
     if we are to be happy, holy people.
For this law is written into our very hearts
     by God!
We will ultimately be judged and known
     by how we respond to what we hear
     in the depths of our consciences.
There we stand alone with God,
     for who can know God's heart?
     and who but we can know how God directs our lives?
But this we do know:
     whatever God directs us to
         will be loving and holy
         as the Church teaches us.
It will never be violent, hateful, or ugly.
For God is love,
     and we are to live as God's children
     which is to live in the light of God's love.
(Article 16)

From the word of the Church.

All   **Thanks be to God for this teaching.**

Prayer of the Church

Leader   O God, of power and might,

All   **Lead us to the truth we pray.**

Leader   You have given us an inner light
so that we might know your will and follow it.

All	**Let your light shine within us.**
Leader	And you have led us to the Church whose precepts protect us from error.
All	**May our souls be formed in your love.**
Leader	May we be faithful to your word
All	**Received in our hearts.** **Amen.**

Blessing

Leader	May God who loves us deeply…
All	**O God, we love you without end.**
Leader	May the Spirit who is our guide…
All	**O Spirit, we listen to your voice.**
Leader	And may Jesus Christ in whose name we gather…
All	**O Jesus, we adore you.**
Leader	now bless us, direct us, and be with us in love, now and forever.
All	**We receive your blessing with full hearts.** **Amen. Amen. Amen.**

Closing Prayer

Leader	(using these or similar words) O God, we know that you are with us and you guide all we are about to do. We are ready now to follow the path you lay for each of us and to recognize your Word within and among us.
All	**In the name of God, Amen.**
Leader	(Invite all to listen to, sing, or recite a closing song-prayer.)

For Other Christians

Leader   (using these or similar words)
Let's all take a moment of silence
here in the midst of our busy lives
    in order to collect the events of today
    and bring ourselves, body and soul,
        into this gathering.

Pause for a moment of sacred silence.

Leader   (using these or similar words)
Friends, we now gather here as God's family,
in solidarity with people of every Christian church
    seeking unity and peace.
May we enter into this time now
    conscious of our high calling
    and open to God's voice within and among us.

All   **In the name of God, Amen.**

Leader   (Invite all to listen to, sing, or recite an opening song-prayer.)

First Reading

Reader   A reading from the Gospel of John (Jn 17:20–23)
"I ask not only on behalf of these, but also on behalf of those who will believe in me through their word, that they may all be one. As you, Father, are in me and I am in you, may they also be in us, so that the world may believe that you have sent me. The glory that you have given me I have given them, so that they may be one, as we are one, I in them and you in me, that they may become completely one, so that the world may know that you have sent me and have loved them even as you have loved me."

The word of the Lord.

All   **Thanks be to God for these words of Scripture!**

Second Reading

Reader A reflection based on The Decree of Ecumenism
from the Second Vatican Council:

To restore unity among Christians
   was one of the chief aims
   of Vatican II.
After all, Christ did not establish two or three
   or a dozen Churches,
   but only one:
      unified, holy, and apostolic.
We have strayed from that unity
   and now is the time for us
   to do what we believe Christ intended:
      to come together as one.
We take this work very seriously
   because we believe it grows directly
   from the heart of the Lord.
And besides that,
   our disunity and competition
   is a scandal to the world!
Why should anyone believe in God's love
   when we who are in the Church
   do not love each other well?

We believe that in these days
   God is working among us
   to bring unity about.
There are signs all around us!

We see now before us the chance
   to become one visible Church of God,
   a community around the world
   that witnesses to God's love.
(Article 1)

From the word of the Church.

All **Thanks be to God for this teaching.**

Prayers for the Church (choose one or compose one):

Leader Jesus, Lord and Giver of Life,
we come to you in faith seeking your grace.

All	**We come in faith.**
Leader	Empower us to know your will and serve you faithfully.
All	**Let your Holy Spirit abide with us now.** **Let your power fill us.**
Leader	Guide all Christian people to the unity you desire for us.
All	**Form us with your word to be your people.**
Leader	End hatred, fighting, and competition among us
All	**And let your love rule our lives.** **Amen.**

Blessing

Leader	May God who loves us deeply…
All	**O God, we love you without end.**
Leader	May the Spirit who is our guide…
All	**O Spirit, we listen to your voice.**
Leader	And may Jesus Christ in whose name we gather…
All	**O Jesus, we adore you.**
Leader	now bless us, direct us, and be with us in love, now and forever.
All	**We receive your blessing with full hearts.** **Amen. Amen. Amen.**

Closing Prayer

Leader	(using these or similar words) O God, we know that you are with us and you guide all we are about to do. We are ready now to join in unity with all

who profess your name.

All   **In the name of God, Amen.**

Leader   (Invite all to listen to, sing, or recite a closing song-prayer.)

For the Jews and People of Other Faiths

Leader   (using these or similar words)
Let's all take a moment of silence
here in the midst of our busy lives
    in order to collect the events of today
    and bring ourselves, body and soul,
        into this gathering.

Pause for a moment of sacred silence.

Leader   (using these or similar words)
Friends, we now gather here as God's family,
gathered with all those who follow their beliefs
    around the world and here at home,
    forming one great human family.
May we enter into this time now
    conscious of our high calling
    and open to God's voice within and among us.

All   **In the name of God, Amen.**

Leader   (Invite all to listen to, sing, or recite an opening song-prayer.)

First Reading

Reader   A reading from the Book of Ezekiel   (Ez 36:24–28)
I will take you from the nations, and gather you from all the countries, and bring you into your own land. I will sprinkle clean water upon you, and you shall be clean from all your uncleannesses, and from all your idols I will cleanse you. A new heart I will give you, and a new spirit I will put within you; and I will remove from your body the heart of stone and give you a heart of flesh. I will put my spirit within you, and make you follow my statutes and be careful to observe my ordinances. Then you shall live in the land that I gave to your ancestors; and you shall be my people, and I will be your God.

The word of the Lord.

All   **Thanks be to God for these words of Scripture!**

Second Reading

Reader: A reflection based on the Declaration on the Relation of the Church to Non-Christian Religions from the Second Vatican Council:

It has always been true
    that among certain people
    there is found an awareness
        of a hidden power
        which guides their lives and events.
This power is expressed
    through their teachings,
    their ways of life,
    and their own sacred ceremonies.
This results in a deeply religious way of life
    for them
    and we do not reject anything in this
        which is true and holy.
In fact, we offer them our own deep esteem
    and we join them in the eternal search for truth.
This does not diminish our proclamation of Christ
    as the way, the truth, and the life.
But it does lead us to dialogue,
    mutual respect,
    and charity for all.
(Article 2)

From the word of the Church.

All   **Thanks be to God for this teaching.**

Prayer of the Church

Leader   O God, you are the one we love with all our heart.

All   **With all our heart.**

Leader   And you are the one whose voice we have heard.

All   **Hear now the prayers of our hearts.**

Leader   We pray in solidarity with all who believe everywhere in the world.

All   **May all live in peace.**

Leader	And we pray for an end to persecution and hatred based on religious differences.
All	**May all live in love.**
Leader	And finally we pray for enlightenment.
All	**Lead all people to truth. Amen.**

Blessing

Leader	May God who loves us deeply…
All	**O God, we love you without end.**
Leader	May the Spirit who is our guide…
All	**O Spirit, we listen to your voice.**
Leader	And may Jesus Christ in whose name we gather…
All	**O Jesus, we adore you.**
Leader	now bless us, direct us, and be with us in love, now and forever.
All	**We receive your blessing with full hearts. Amen. Amen. Amen.**

Closing Prayer

Leader	(using these or similar words) O God, we know that you are with us and you guide all we are about to do. We are ready now to stand shoulder to shoulder with people of every Faith to build a human family in peace and love.
All	**In the name of God, Amen.**
Leader	(Invite all to listen to, sing, or recite a closing song-prayer.)

For the Ministry of our Clergy

Leader	(using these or similar words)
	Let's all take a moment of silence
	here in the midst of our busy lives
	in order to collect the events of today
	and bring ourselves, body and soul,
	into this gathering.

Pause for a moment of sacred silence.

Leader	(using these or similar words)
	Friends, we now gather here as God's family,
	the people brought into unity as a Church
	with the Bishop of Rome
	and our own bishops as well.
	May we enter into this time now
	conscious of our high calling
	and open to God's voice within and among us.

All	**In the name of God, Amen.**

Leader	(Invite all to listen to, sing, or recite an opening song-prayer.)

First Reading

Reader	A reading from the Gospel of Mark (Mk 1:16–20)
	As Jesus passed along the Sea of Galilee, he saw Simon and his brother Andrew casting a net into the sea—for they were fishermen. And Jesus said to them, "Follow me and I will make you fish for people." And immediately they left their nets and followed him. As he went a little farther, he saw James son of Zebedee and his brother John, who were in their boat mending the nets. Immediately he called them; and they left their father Zebedee in the boat with the hired men, and followed him.
	The word of the Lord.

All	**Thanks be to God for these words of Scripture!**

Second Reading

Reader   A reflection based on The Dogmatic Constitution on the Church
from the Second Vatican Council:

Before appointing the first twelve apostles,
      Jesus prayed at length for insight.
These first apostles formed a community with him
      and would come eventually to provide
        the leadership needed to proclaim the Gospel
          faithfully to the world.
Peter stood at their head.

At Pentecost, the Holy Spirit confirmed them
      in this mission
      which has lasted down through time
        to our own very day
        and will continue to the end of the world.
Thus did the church preach,
      heal,
      minister,
      and proclaim in the name of Christ
        to all the world . . .
Eventually these leaders were called "bishops."
(Article 19)

The divinely established ministries of the Church
      are carried on day to day
      by people in various roles
      called bishops, priests, and deacons.
Priests, for their part,
      are consecrated in the image of Christ
      to preach and guide the faithful
        entrusted to their care.
The most important role they play
      is to preside at the Eucharist
      where they stand in solidarity with their bishop
        connected to Christ
        and leading all the people.
(Article 28)

For their part, deacons have a ministry of service
      to preside at baptism,
      to distribute the Eucharist,
      to bless marriages,
      to bring Viaticum to the sick and dying,
      to bury the dead,

and to assist with the administration of the Church.
(Article 29)

From the word of the Church.

All **Thanks be to God for this teaching.**

Prayer of the Church

Leader In the beginning, O God, you established order
in the midst of the chaos of creation.

All **Send holy order to your church through
the bishops and clergy.**

Leader You led us through the desert with a pillar of light.

All **Now lead us through these times with
the light of your word.**

Leader And you gave us Jesus Christ as our own.

All **May our bishops stand among us as ones who
serve Christ faithfully.
Amen.**

Blessing

Leader May God who loves us deeply…

All **O God, we love you without end.**

Leader May the Spirit who is our guide…

All **O Spirit, we listen to your voice.**

Leader And may Jesus Christ in whose name we gather…

All **O Jesus, we adore you.**

Leader now bless us,
direct us,
and be with us in love, now and forever.

All   We receive your blessing with full hearts.
             Amen. Amen. Amen.

Closing Prayer

Leader   (using these or similar words)
             O God, we know that you are with us
             and you guide all we are about to do.
             We are ready now to gather in unity
                     with our bishops and clergy
                         around the world and here at home.

All   In the name of God, Amen.

Leader   (Invite all to listen to, sing, or recite a closing song-prayer.)

For Religious Women and Men

Leader   (using these or similar words)
Let's all take a moment of silence
here in the midst of our busy lives
    in order to collect the events of today
    and bring ourselves, body and soul,
        into this gathering.

Pause for a moment of sacred silence.

Leader   (using these or similar words)
Friends, we now gather here as God's family,
together with those women and men
    who have dedicated their lives to Christ
    in religious vows.
May we enter into this time now
    conscious of our high calling
    and open to God's voice within and among us.

All   **In the name of God, Amen.**

Leader   (Invite all to listen to, sing, or recite an opening song-prayer.)

First Reading

Reader   A reading from the Gospel of Luke (Lk 4:16–21)
When he came to Nazareth, where he had been brought up, he went to the synagogue on the sabbath day, as was his custom. He stood up to read, and the scroll of the prophet Isaiah was given to him. He unrolled the scroll and found the place where it was written: "The Spirit of the Lord is upon me, because he has anointed me to bring good news to the poor. He has sent me to proclaim release to the captives and recovery of sight to the blind, to let the oppressed go free, to proclaim the year of the Lord's favor." And he rolled up the scroll, gave it back to the attendant, and sat down. The eyes of all in the synagogue were fixed on him. Then he began to say to them, "Today this scripture has been fulfilled in your hearing."

The word of the Lord.

All   **Thanks be to God for these words of Scripture!**

Second Reading

Reader   A reflection based on the Dogmatic Constitution on the Church
from the Second Vatican Council:

Those who enter religious life
     make solemn vows or promises
     dedicating themselves wholly to God.
Even though at baptism they died to sin
     and committed themselves to love,
     religious vows allow them
        to deepen their baptismal commitment
        and live entirely for God.
This gives them freedom
     and consecrates them to God's work,
     whatever that work may be.
(Article 44)

From the word of the Church.

All   **Thanks be to God for this teaching.**

Prayers for the Church   (choose one or compose one):

Leader   Lord of the Universe, we now bring our needs to you.

All   **We come to you with our needs.**
Hear us O Lord.

Leader   We celebrate now the men and women among us
who have given their lives entirely to you
in religious communities around the world.

All   **May the example of their lives and the labor of**
their hands build up the body of Christ everywhere.

Leader   May all of us follow their example of Faith
and live in solidarity with you and the Gospel you proclaim.

All   **And may we do this work in love.**
Amen.

Blessing

Leader	May God who loves us deeply…
All	**O God, we love you without end.**
Leader	May the Spirit who is our guide…
All	**O Spirit, we listen to your voice.**
Leader	And may Jesus Christ in whose name we gather…
All	**O Jesus, we adore you.**
Leader	now bless us, direct us, and be with us in love, now and forever.
All	**We receive your blessing with full hearts. Amen. Amen. Amen.**

Closing Prayer

Leader	(using these or similar words)
	O God, we know that you are with us
	and you guide all we are about to do.
	May many more women and men be led
	     to a full commitment of their lives
	     in service to the Gospel.

All	**In the name of God, Amen.**
Leader	(Invite all to listen to, sing, or recite a closing song-prayer.)

For the Priesthood and Vocations to Holy Orders

Leader   (using these or similar words)
Let's all take a moment of silence
here in the midst of our busy lives
     in order to collect the events of today
     and bring ourselves, body and soul,
          into this gathering.

Pause for a moment of sacred silence.

Leader   (using these or similar words)
Friends, we now gather here as God's family,
     priests, religious, and laypeople.
May we enter into this time now
     conscious of own high calling
  and open to God's voice within and among us.

All   **In the name of God, Amen.**

Leader   (Invite all to listen to, sing, or recite an opening song-prayer.)

First Reading

Reader   A reading from the Gospel of Luke (Lk 22:15–20)
He said to them, "I have eagerly desired to eat this Passover with you before I suffer; for I tell you, I will not eat it until it is fulfilled in the kingdom of God." Then he took a cup, and after giving thanks he said, "Take this and divide it among yourselves; for I tell you that from now on I will not drink of the fruit of the vine until the kingdom of God comes." Then he took a loaf of bread, and when he had given thanks, he broke it and gave it to them, saying, "This is my body, which is given for you. Do this in remembrance of me." And he did the same with the cup after supper, saying, "This cup that is poured out for you is the new covenant in my blood."

The word of the Lord.

All   **Thanks be to God for these words of Scripture!**

Second Reading

Reader   A reflection based on The Decree on the Life and Ministry of Priests
from the Second Vatican Council:

Priests are chosen from the human family
      and are appointed to act on behalf
          of the rest of us
          in order to offer gifts
      and live among us as our brothers.
This is similar to how Christ lived among us.

In order to do their work,
      priests are set apart somewhat
      among the people of God
          but this is only true
          in order to make it possible for them
             to give themselves entirely.
They serve God on one hand,
      but they also serve the Church.
Therefore, they must be in close touch with God
      and also with us.
This is a great challenge
      but they're given a special grace
      which empowers them for their work.
This grace is expressed in their lives
      through their goodness,
      their sincerity and constancy,
      their sense of justice and charity,
      their courtesy and kindness.
(Article 3)

From the word of the Church.

All   **Thanks be to God for this teaching.**

Prayer of the Church

Leader   O God, you have given the gift of the priesthood
to us, the Church.

All   **Now we pray for our priests.**

Leader   May those called to this vocation
be people of holiness and grace.

All	**May they be dedicated to the truth.**
Leader	May they find in the Church the support they need to sustain their difficult work
All	**And lead them to their own personal holiness. Amen.**

Blessing

Leader	May God who loves us deeply…
All	**O God, we love you without end.**
Leader	May the Spirit who is our guide…
All	**O Spirit, we listen to your voice.**
Leader	And may Jesus Christ in whose name we gather…
All	**O Jesus, we adore you.**
Leader	now bless us, direct us, and be with us in love, now and forever.
All	**We receive your blessing with full hearts. Amen. Amen. Amen.**

Closing Prayer

Leader	(using these or similar words)
	O God, we know that you are with us
	and you guide all we are about to do.
	We are ready now to love and care for the priests
	     of our Church
	        so they may serve you more faithfully
	        and lead our parish communities to Christ.

All	**In the name of God, Amen.**
Leader	(Invite all to listen to, sing, or recite a closing song-prayer.)

Vatican II
Prayer for Justice

Leader   (using these or similar words)
Let's all take a moment of silence
here in the midst of our busy lives
      in order to collect the events of today
      and bring ourselves, body and soul,
         into this gathering.

Pause for a moment of sacred silence.

Leader   (using these or similar words)
Friends, we now gather here as God's family,
      the people chosen to establish justice on earth
      in your name.
May we enter into this time now
      conscious of our high calling
      and open to God's voice within and among us.

All   **In the name of God, Amen.**

Leader   (Invite all to listen to, sing, or recite an opening song-prayer.)

First Reading

Reader   A reading from the Gospel of Luke (Lk 11:42–46)
"But woe to you Pharisees! For you tithe mint and rue and herbs of all kinds, and neglect justice and the love of God; it is these you ought to have practiced, without neglecting the others. Woe to you Pharisees! For you love to have the seat of honor in the synagogues and to be greeted with respect in the marketplaces. Woe to you! For you are like unmarked graves, and people walk over them without realizing it."

One of the lawyers answered him, "Teacher, when you say these things, you insult us too." And he said, "Woe also to you lawyers! For you load people with burdens hard to bear, and you yourselves do not lift a finger to ease them."

The word of the Lord.

All   **Thanks be to God for these words of Scripture!**

Second Reading

Reader   A reflection based on the Pastoral Constitution on the Church
in the Modern World from the Second Vatican Council:

The first requirement
      if peace is to succeed in our time,
      is to end the causes of discord
            which lead people to war.
This means, concretely,
      that economic justice is needed,
      that the desire for power is tamed,
      and that selfish passions
            are identified and controlled.
In order for this to occur,
      we must learn to
      share this planet together in peace.
We must create a system of governance
      which meets the needs
      of today's people.

Certain international bodies must be allowed
      to take their proper role
      in assisting the world
            to find peace through justice.
Christians and those of other world religions
      are working more together
      and we applaud this!
(Articles 83 & 84)

From the word of the Church.

All   **Thanks be to God for this teaching.**

Prayer of the Church

Leader   O God, you are the maker of justice,
and you teach us to treat one another in love.

All   **Make us people of justice, we pray.**

Leader   Now we offer ourselves to do your work in the world,
the work of announcing your Reign

All   **And establishing your justice for all people.**

Leader	For this we need your grace, your wisdom, your courage, and your power. For this we need eyes of faith.
All	**May we see the world as you do and may we not rest until justice is done. Amen. Amen. Amen.**

Blessing

Leader	May God who loves us deeply…
All	**O God, we love you without end.**
Leader	May the Spirit who is our guide…
All	**O Spirit, we listen to your voice.**
Leader	And may Jesus Christ in whose name we gather…
All	**O Jesus, we adore you.**
Leader	now bless us, direct us, and be with us in love, now and forever.
All	**We receive your blessing with full hearts. Amen. Amen. Amen.**

Closing Prayer

Leader	(using these or similar words)
	O God, we know that you are with us
	and you guide all we are about to do.
	We are ready now to be people of justice and peace,
	    to work tirelessly so that your Reign
	        may be announced and your justice made known.

All	**In the name of God, Amen.**
Leader	(Invite all to listen to, sing, or recite a closing song-prayer.)

Vatican II
Prayer for Peace

Leader   (using these or similar words)
Let's all take a moment of silence
here in the midst of our busy lives
    in order to collect the events of today
    and bring ourselves, body and soul,
        into this gathering.

Pause for a moment of sacred silence.

Leader   (using these or similar words)
Friends, we now gather here as God's family,
    called to be peacemakers in today's world.
May we enter into this time now
    conscious of our high calling
    and open to God's voice within and among us.

All   **In the name of God, Amen.**

Leader   (Invite all to listen to, sing, or recite an opening song-prayer.)

First Reading

Reader   A reading from the second letter of Paul to the Corinthians (2 Cor 13:11–12)
Finally, brothers and sisters, farewell. Put things in order, listen to my appeal,
agree with one another, live in peace; and the God of love and peace will be with
you. Greet one another with a holy kiss. All the saints greet you. The grace of the
Lord Jesus Christ, the love of God, and the communion of the Holy Spirit be with
all of you.

The word of the Lord.

All   **Thanks be to God for these words of Scripture!**

Second Reading

Reader   A reflection based on Pastoral Constitution on the Church
in the Modern World from the Second Vatican Council:

Peace is more than the absence of war,
　　more than the maintenance
　　of a balance of power between enemies.
It is more than the firm hold of a dictator
　　that, for the moment, involves no bloodshed.
But then, what is peace?

We believe that peace is the result of justice.
When society is rightly ordered,
　　when people live as God intends,
　　then peace reigns.
But while this is true,
　　we also realize that peace
　　must be constantly built up,
　　　　human nature must be called
　　　　again and again to make peace.
But even this is not sufficient.

We believe, further,
　　that peace comes, in the end, from love.
Unless people willingly come together
　　to share their talents and bright minds,
　　peace cannot be achieved.
Love goes beyond what justice can achieve.

When we love our neighbor,
　　even those who irritate us
　　or alienate us,
　　　　then we give peace its only chance.
All of this loving attitude and behavior
　　connect us to Christ
　　who is the only one who can bring real peace.
Forgo violence,
　　speak with love,
　　and defend the weak—
　　　　for then you are in Christ
　　　　and the peace of the world is at hand.
(Article 78)

From the word of the Church.

All　　　　　**Thanks be to God for this teaching.**

Prayer of the Church

Leader　　　　O Mary, Queen of Peace,

we stand in solidarity with you and Jesus Christ, your son.

All   **Help us see the way to peace.**

Leader   Guide us, we pray, to be conscious of our world
                 and its many needs.

All   **Give us the courage to witness to Christ.**

Leader   In all we say and do, may we be people of peace,

All   **In our homes, our communities, and our nations.**

Leader   Stir up within us the desire to take the actions needed
                 to establish peace on earth in these days of turmoil and hatred
                 no matter what personal cost there may be in doing so.

All   **May we do this work in love and faith.**
                 Amen.

Blessing

Leader   May God who loves us deeply…

All   **O God, we love you without end.**

Leader   May the Spirit who is our guide…

All   **O Spirit, we listen to your voice.**

Leader   And may Jesus Christ in whose name we gather…

All   **O Jesus, we adore you.**

Leader   now bless us,
                 direct us,
                 and be with us in love, now and forever.

All   **We receive your blessing with full hearts.**
                 Amen. Amen. Amen.

Closing Prayer

Leader   (using these or similar words)
                 O God, we know that you are with us

and that you guide all we are about to do.
We are ready now to be people of peace
and to witness Christ's peace to the world
despite the risks we may bear.

All   **In the name of God, Amen.**

Leader   (Invite all to listen to, sing, or recite a closing song-prayer.)

For Lay Leadership in the Parish

Leader   (using these or similar words)
Let's all take a moment of silence
here in the midst of our busy lives
      in order to collect the events of today
      and bring ourselves, body and soul,
         into this gathering.

Pause for a moment of sacred silence.

Leader   (using these or similar words)
Friends, we now gather here as God's family,
the people chosen to work in our parishes
      and minister to one another.
May we enter into this time now
      conscious of our high calling
      and open to God's voice within and among us.

All   **In the name of God, Amen.**

Leader   (Invite all to listen to, sing, or recite an opening song-prayer.)

First Reading

Reader   A reading from the Gospel of Matthew (Mt 9:36–38)
When he saw the crowds, he had compassion for them, because they were harassed and helpless, like sheep without a shepherd. Then he said to his disciples, "The harvest is plentiful, but the laborers are few; therefore ask the Lord of the harvest to send out laborers into his harvest."

The word of the Lord.

All   **Thanks be to God for these words of Scripture!**

Second Reading

Reader   A reflection based on the Decree on the Apostolate of the Laity
from the Second Vatican Council:

We at the Second Vatican Council
    make an earnest appeal
    to all the laypeople of the Church.
We ask that you make a willing,
    noble,
    and enthusiastic response to God's call.
Christ is calling you indeed!
    The Spirit is urging you.
You who are in the younger generation:
    you, too, are being called!
Welcome this call with an eager heart
    and a generous spirit.
It is the Lord, through this council,
    who is once more inviting all Christians
    of every level of the Church
        to work diligently in the harvest.
Join yourselves to the mission of Christ
    in the world,
    knowing that in the Lord,
        your labors will not be lost.
(Article 33)

From the word of the Church.

All   **Thanks be to God for this teaching.**

Prayer of the Church

Leader   O God, of goodness and love
we pray in gratitude for the laity of the Church.

All   **May your wisdom and courage lead the laity
to a ministry of compassion.**

Leader   We believe that each baptized person
is called to work for your Reign on Earth

All   **and called by you to witness in love.**

Leader   Now we pray that the church will be blessed
with countless workers and generous hearts

All   **to do your work on earth and lead
all people to holiness.**

Leader   We pray in the name of Christ.

All	Amen. Again we say, Amen!

Blessing

Leader	May God who loves us deeply…
All	**O God, we love you without end.**
Leader	May the Spirit who is our guide…
All	**O Spirit, we listen to your voice.**
Leader	And may Jesus Christ in whose name we gather…
All	**O Jesus, we adore you.**
Leader	now bless us, direct us, and be with us in love, now and forever.
All	**We receive your blessing with full hearts. Amen. Amen. Amen.**

Closing Prayer

Leader	(using these or similar words) O God, we know that you are with us and you guide all we are about to do. We are ready now to minister in your name and to make our parish a sign to the world of your love.
All	**In the name of God, Amen.**
Leader	(Invite all to listen to, sing, or recite a closing song-prayer.)

For Lay Leadership in the World

Leader   (using these or similar words)
Let's all take a moment of silence
here in the midst of our busy lives
    in order to collect the events of today
    and bring ourselves, body and soul,
      into this gathering.

Pause for a moment of sacred silence.

Leader   (using these or similar words)
Friends, we now gather here as God's family,
    the people chosen to bring God's love to the world.
May we enter into this time now
    conscious of our high calling
    and open to God's voice within and among us.

All   **In the name of God, Amen.**

Leader   (Invite all to listen to, sing, or recite an opening song-prayer.)

First Reading

Reader   A reading from the Gospel of Matthew (Mt 5:13–16)
"You are the salt of the earth; but if salt has lost its taste, how can its saltiness be restored? It is no longer good for anything, but is thrown out and trampled under foot. You are the light of the world. A city built on a hill cannot be hid. No one after lighting a lamp puts it under the bushel basket, but on the lampstand, and it gives light to all in the house. In the same way, let your light shine before others, so that they may see your good works and give glory to your Father in heaven."

The word of the Lord.

All   **Thanks be to God for these words of Scripture!**

Second Reading

Reader   A reflection based on the Decree on the Apostolate of the Laity
from the Second Vatican Council:

There are diverse ministries
      within the Church
      but there is only one mission.
While bishops and clergy are charged
      with teaching, sanctifying and governing,
      laypeople, too, have an essential role
         in the mission of Christ.
Indeed, laypeople share in the
      priestly,
      prophetic,
      and royal role of Christ.
Concretely, this means
      that laypeople are called to
      help lead others to holiness.
Laypeople are called
      to help animate the world
      with the spirit of Christ.
In fact, it is true that laypeople
      are called to be salt for the earth
      and light for the world!
(Article 2)

From the word of the Church.

All   **Thanks be to God for this teaching.**

Prayer of the Church

Leader   We know, O God, that this world needs your Love
to guide and sustain it.

All   **Help us, we pray, to transform the world in your name.**

Leader   You give us all we need:
every gift, every talent, every opportunity
and you put before us the task of using these gifts

All   **To lead all people to your heart.**

Leader   We pray now for the courage to do this work

All	For we know we need your grace. **Amen.**

Blessing

Leader	May God who loves us deeply…
All	**O God, we love you without end.**
Leader	May the Spirit who is our guide…
All	**O Spirit, we listen to your voice.**
Leader	And may Jesus Christ in whose name we gather…
All	**O Jesus, we adore you.**
Leader	now bless us, direct us, and be with us in love, now and forever.
All	**We receive your blessing with full hearts. Amen. Amen. Amen.**

Closing Prayer

Leader	(using these or similar words) O God, we know that you are with us and you guide all we are about to do. We are ready now to undertake the work of transforming the world in God's love.
All	**In the name of God, Amen.**
Leader	(Invite all to listen to, sing, or recite a closing song-prayer.)

Vatican II
Annotated Reading and Resource List

The Actual Documents

Vatican Council II
        Austin Flannery, OP
Available as a revised translation in inclusive language. (Dublin: Dominican, 1996)

Summaries of the Actual Documents

Vatican II in Plain English
        Bill Huebsch
A three-volume set that includes *The Council, The Constitutions,* and *The Decrees and Declarations.* This work is unique because it offers a summary of all sixteen council documents in engaging sense lines. A timeline of church history and helpful bibliography are included. (Allen, TX: Thomas More, 1996)

General Works on the Council

Destination Vatican II (CD/ROM)
For use in a school computer lab or home computer, this is technology that touches the heart. An interactive format allows learners to tour St. Peter's Square, view actual council footage, and interview council participants. The original council documents, *Vatican Council II* by Xavier Rynne, and the *Council Daybooks,* plus Bill Huebsch's *Vatican II in Plain English* are included with full word search, print, and "hot text" capability. Available in PC and MAC formats. (Allen, TX: Thomas More, 1997)

Vatican Council II
        Xavier Rynne
This is a detailed account of the proceedings of the council itself and is still the best for accuracy, style, and astute observation. This version is a condensed edition of Rynne's four volumes, one for each session of Vatican II. Available on *Destination Vatican II* CD-ROM (Allen, TX: Thomas More, 1997) or from a used bookstore.

A Concise History of the Catholic Church
        Thomas Bokenkotter
There is simply no better, more objective postconciliar history of the church than this one for readability and indexing. (New York: Doubleday Image Books, 1990)

The Church Emerging from Vatican II
        Dennis M. Doyle
This is a well-written and easy-to-read treatment of how the council affected the day-to-day life of the church. This book makes wide use of anecdotes and stories as a way of situating the council in today's church. (Mystic, CT: Twenty-Third Publications, 1992)

Council Daybook (three volumes)
        Edited by Floyd Anderson
For the most complete story of the council's proceedings from the opening speeches to a closing bell, read this. It can easily be browsed and has an extremely complete index if one is looking for something specific. It is out of print but available in used bookstores or on the *Destination Vatican II* CD-ROM. (Allen, TX: Thomas More, 1997)

The Faithful Revolution
A 5-video, historical documentary on the Second Vatican Council, the Church's "defining moment" of the second millennium. This video series includes a study guide which can be used in parish and school settings. *Blackline Masters* are also available to supplement school and parish courses. (Allen, TX: Thomas More, 1997)

Praying with Pope John XXIII
Written by William Huebsch this work will put you in touch with Pope John's spirituality and vision. It will become an invaluable prayer guide for you. (Winona, MN: St. Mary's Press, 1999)

Guests in Their Own House: The Women of Vatican II
An honest and sometimes painful-to-read history of the women who were present for the council, much of it in their own words. The author, Carmel McEnroy, has researched this book very well and it's an important link in understanding, in part, what Vatican II did *not* do. (New York: Crossroad, 1996)

History of Vatican II, Vols 1 and 2
The first major and exhaustive history of the council. Not an easy read but essential to anyone who wants to fully understand the provenance of the various documents and conciliar activities. Edited by Giuseppe Alberigo and Joseph Komonchak. (Maryknoll, NY: Orbis and Leuven: Petters, 1995 and 1996 respectively)

The Theology of the Council in Common Language
following titles by William Huebsch

A Spirituality of Wholeness: A New Look at Grace
Gives a good treatment of Rahner's theology of grace which was a major theological shift which influenced the council. (Mystic, CT: Twenty-Third Publications, 1988)

Rethinking Sacraments: Holy Moments in Daily Living
Summarizes the shift in sacramental theology and practice which the council launched in its constitution on the Liturgy. (Mystic, CT: Twenty-Third Publications, 1989)

A New Look at Prayer: Searching for Bliss
Helps the reader come to understand the place of grace and sacrament in personal prayer. (Mystic, CT: Twenty-Third Publications, 1991)

A Radical Guide for Catholics
Provides a summary of the council's treatment on conscience and then applies it with story and reflection to several modern situations. (Mystic, CT: Twenty-Third Publications, 1992)

Also by Bill Huebsch

Handbook for Success in Whole Community Catechesis

Here is a resource destined to become the bible of whole community catechesis! Popular author Bill Huebsch lays out the principles of whole community catechesis, offers practical steps that focus first on conversion and then on catechesis, develops suggestions and ideas for fostering households of faith, and presents several models of how whole community catechesis can work in a parish—all written in simple to understand language and a sense line format. The book contains extensive reproducible pages for use in the parish, home, or school.   953083, $19.95

The General Directory for Catechesis in Plain English
A Summary and Commentary

Provides an outstanding paraphrase of the Directory with a brief study guide in the front to help readers ask thoughtful questions and focus on key points as they study the text.   951331, $10.95

People of God at Prayer
18 Services in the Spirit of Vatican II

These beautifully written prayer services, based on the major themes of Vatican II, celebrate a universal call to holiness and focus on the powerful work of the Spirit in the Church.   950122, $12.95

A New Look at Grace
A Spirituality of Wholeness

Bill Huebsch's distinctive prose images and storytelling create an unforgettable journey to the mystery and wonder of the "other side" of our everyday experiences. Here we discover anew the power and beauty of God's grace.   223558, $12.95

Heritage of Faith
A Framework for Whole Community Catechesis
Jo Rotunno

Jo Rotunno suggests that for parish-wide catechesis to be effective, a structured scope and sequence of content be incorporated into programs for parish members of all ages. She then provides seven sample seasonal/doctrinal themes that are connected to the lectionary but not bound to it Sunday by Sunday. In addition she offers Questions of the Week for every week of all three years of the liturgical cycle, to foster the sharing of the Word that is at the heart of whole community catechesis.   953091, $12.95

TWENTY-THIRD PUBLICATIONS

185 WILLOW STREET • PO BOX 180 • MYSTIC, CT 06355
TEL: 1-800-321-0411 • FAX: 1-800-572-0788
Bayard   E-MAIL: ttpubs@aol.com • www.twentythirdpublications.com